OPRAH WINFREY

An Inspiration to Millions

by Wil Mara

Content Consultant

Nanci R. Vargus, Ed.D.
Professor Emeritus, University of Indianapolis

Reading Consultant

Jeanne M. Clidas, Ph.D.

Children's Press®
An Imprint of Scholastic Inc.

Library of Congress Cataloging-in-Publication Data
Names: Mara, Wil, author.
Title: Oprah Winfrey : an inspiration to millions / by Wil Mara ; poem by Jodie Shepherd.
Description: New York : Children's Press, an imprint of Scholastic, Inc.,
[2017] | Series: Rookie biographies | Includes bibliographical references and index.
Identifiers: LCCN 2016003495| ISBN 9780531216835 (reinforced library binding)
| ISBN 9780531217665 (pbk. : alk. paper)
Subjects: LCSH: Winfrey, Oprah—Juvenile literature. | Television personalities—United
States—Biography—Juvenile literature. | African American television personalities–
Biography–Juvenile literature. | Actors—United States—Biography—Juvenile literature.
| African American actors—Biography—Juvenile literature.
Classification: LCC PN1992.4.W56 M373 2017 | DDC 791.4502/8092–dc23 LC
record available at http://lccn.loc.gov/2016003495

Produced by Spooky Cheetah Press
Poem by Jodie Shepherd

© 2017 by Scholastic Inc.

Printed in China 62

SCHOLASTIC, CHILDREN'S PRESS, ROOKIE BIOGRAPHIES™, and associated logos are
trademarks and/or registered trademarks of Scholastic Inc.

1 2 3 4 5 6 7 8 9 10 R 25 24 23 22 21 20 19 18 17 16

Photographs ©: cover background: Godruma/Thinkstock; cover main: Jim Smeal/BEI/
Shutterstock/Rex USA; 3 background: Dean Pictures/Newscom; 4-5: Scott Barbour/
Getty Images; 7 background: daboost/Thinkstock; 7 main: Supplied by PacificCoastNews/
Newscom; 9: Everett Collection; 10-11: Charlie Knoblock/AP Images; 12: Kevin Horan/
Corbis Images; 14-15: George Widman/AP Images; 16: Jim Smeal/BEI/REX/Shutterstock/
Reuters; 17: Tim Boyle/Getty Images; 18-19: Gallo Images/Rex Features/AP Images;
20-21 left: George Burns Feature Photo Service/Newscom; 21 right: John Fitzhugh/
MCT/Newscom; 23: Nancy Kaszerman/ZUMA Press/Newscom; 24-25: yellowpaul/
Getty Images; 26-27: Kevin Dietsch/UPI/Newscom; 29: Noam Galai/Getty Images;
30: DeshaCAM/Shutterstock, Inc.; 31 top: George Burns Feature Photo Service/
Newscom; 31 center top: Jim Smeal/BEI/REX/Shutterstock/Reuters; 31 center bottom:
George Widman/AP Images; 31 bottom: Everett Collection; 32: Dean Pictures/Newscom.

Maps by Mapping Specialists

TABLE OF CONTENTS

Meet
Oprah Winfrey

When Oprah Winfrey was growing up, women were not expected to be successful. They rarely had the chance! But Oprah dared to dream big. She proved that, with hard work and **perseverance**, anything is possible.

Oprah Gail Winfrey was born on January 29, 1954, in Kosciusko, Mississippi. Her father left home before Oprah was born. She and her mother had very little money. Other kids made fun of Oprah for being so poor. That made her determined to become successful.

FAST FACT!

Oprah's first name is actually "Orpah." But many people who knew her pronounced it "Oprah." So that became the name she used.

This is a photo of a very young Oprah with her mother.

CANADA

UNITED STATES

■ Nashville

● Kosciusko

MEXICO

MAP KEY

● City where Oprah
Winfrey was born

■ City where Oprah
Winfrey lived

Area
enlarged

When Oprah was a teenager, she went to live with her father in Nashville, Tennessee. He was strict, but very caring. Oprah's father taught her the importance of a good education. Oprah worked hard in school. She even earned a **scholarship** to college!

Oprah won a beauty contest in high school.

A Star Is Born

While she was still in college, Oprah got a job reading news stories on the radio. People liked listening to Oprah. She was friendly and cheerful. A few years later, Oprah started reading the news on TV. She also began working on a talk show.

Oprah relaxes in her office at the television studio.

The Oprah Winfrey Show, 1986

In 1983, Oprah moved to Chicago. She became the host of another talk show. In addition to listening to others, Oprah shared her personal stories. She—and the show—became very popular. Soon the name of the show was changed to *The Oprah Winfrey Show*.

FAST FACT!

In 1985, Oprah starred in the movie *The Color Purple*. She was nominated for an Academy Award!

By the 1990s, *The Oprah Winfrey Show* was popular all over the world.

Oprah also got involved in **politics**. She asked the United States Congress to make a new law. The law would protect children from people who might want to hurt them. It was passed in 1994.

Oprah with former presidents Bill Clinton (left) and George H.W. Bush (right)

In 1999, Oprah received a gold medal from the National Book Foundation. The award was for her contributions to reading.

Changing the World

Oprah had always loved to read. She wanted to get everyone to read more books. In 1996, she began Oprah's Book Club. Oprah would choose a book. Then she and other people on her show would talk about it.

Every book chosen for Oprah's club became very popular!

Meanwhile, Oprah was always helping people. She never forgot how hard it was to grow up poor. She wanted to share her good fortune with others. She also wanted to inspire other people to help those in need.

FAST FACT!

Oprah once treated her staff and their families to a trip to Hawaii! She is generous to people who work for her.

Oprah poses with graduates of the Oprah Winfrey Leadership Academy in South Africa.

No. 0023

PAY
TO THE
ORDER OF **The Angel Network** $ 100,000.00

One Hundred Thousand Dollars and ———— 00/100 DOLLARS

Oprah accepts a donation to the Angel Network.

In 1998, Oprah created Oprah's Angel Network. This group of people helped others. Some built schools in poor areas. Others **donated** school supplies to kids who had none.

Money from the Angel Network helped to repair homes that were damaged in a hurricane.

In early 2000, Oprah began publishing a magazine. It is called *O, The Oprah Magazine*. She is always pictured on the cover.

In 2006, Oprah started a radio station called Oprah Radio. She also began writing books. As always, her focus was on inspiring people to live better lives.

Oprah shows off her new magazine at the publication's launch.

Oprah speaks at an event to help sick children.

By the 2010s, Oprah had become one of the most successful people in the world. She was paid more money than any other person on television. She was also the first African-American woman in history to become a billionaire.

A Bright Future

The last episode of *The Oprah Winfrey Show* aired on May 25, 2011. Since then, Oprah has put a lot of time into her other projects.

In 2013, she was awarded the Presidential Medal of Freedom. This is the highest award an American citizen can receive.

President Obama presents Oprah with the Medal of Freedom.

Oprah Winfrey is a true star. She has made a difference in the lives of countless people. She has also proved that, with hard work, ordinary people really can achieve their dreams.

Timeline of Oprah Winfrey's Life

1954	**1983**	**1998**
Born on January 29	*The Oprah Winfrey Show* debuts	Creates Oprah's Angel Network

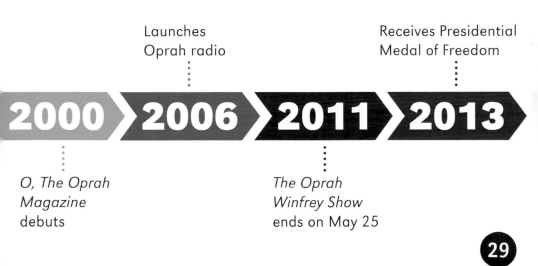

Launches
Oprah radio

Receives Presidential
Medal of Freedom

2000   **2006**   **2011**   **2013**

*O, The Oprah
Magazine*
debuts

*The Oprah
Winfrey Show*
ends on May 25

A Poem About Oprah Winfrey

She grew up poor but had a dream
and worked till it came true.
She inspired many 'round the world
to work on their dreams, too.

You Can Make a Difference

Work hard and always follow your dreams!

Be generous with your time, energy, and talents.

Remember that people who do good things often inspire others to do good things.

Glossary

- **donated** (DOH-nay-ted): gave something to charity

- **perseverance** (pur-suh-VEER-enss): continuing to do something even if it is hard or unlikely to succeed

- **politics** (PAH-li-tiks): activity and discussions involved in governing a country, state, or city

- **scholarship** (SKAHL-ur-ship): money that pays for school

Index

Facts for Now

Visit this Scholastic Web site for more information on Oprah Winfrey:
www.factsfornow.scholastic.com
Enter the keywords Oprah Winfrey

About the Author

Wil Mara first met Oprah Winfrey in 2001 and since then has been a huge fan of her work. He is a best-selling and award-winning author of more than 150 books, many of which are educational titles for children.